I Wonder Why

Countries Fly Flags

and Other Questions About People and Places

Philip Steele

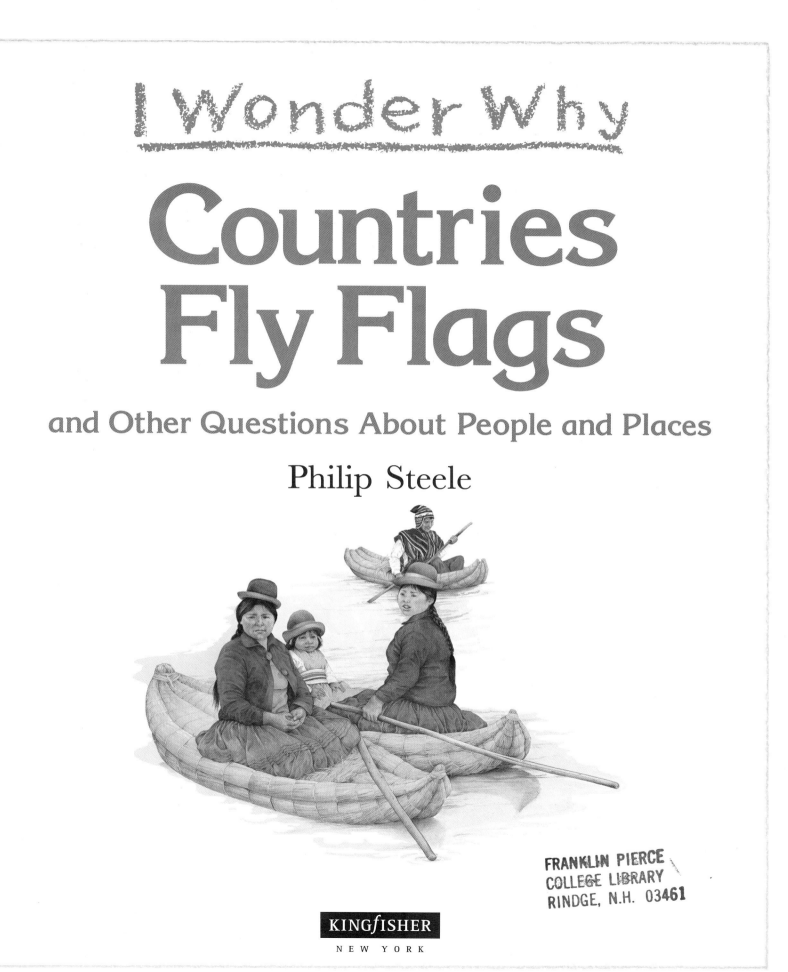

KING*f*ISHER

NEW YORK

KINGFISHER
Larousse Kingfisher Chambers Inc.
95 Madison Avenue
New York, New York 10016

First edition 1995
10 9 8 7 6 5 4 3   (HB)
10 9 8 7 6 5 4 3 2 1 (RLB)
Copyright © Larousse plc 1995

LIBRARY OF CONGRESS CATALOGING-IN-PUBLICATION DATA
Steele, Philip.
    I wonder why countries fly flags and other questions about
peoples and places/by Philip Steele—1st American ed.
        p. cm.
    Includes Index.
    Summary: Answers questions about people, places, and things,
including "Where do elephants glow in the dark?" and "Where
does chocolate grow on trees?"
    1. Manners and peoples. Miscellaneous — Juvenile literature
— [1. Manners and peoples. Miscellaneous. 2. Questions and
answers. I. Title. II. Series: I wonder why (New York, N.Y.)
GT85. S74 1995
395—dc20 94-45211 CIP AC

ISBN 1-85697-582-7 (HB)
ISBN 1-85697-642-4 (RLB)
Printed in Italy

Series editor: Jackie Gaff
Art editor: Christina Fraser
Cover illustrations: Ruby Green, cartoons by Tony Kenyon
    (B.L. Kearley)
Illustrations: Peter Dennis (Linda Rogers Associates);
    Chris Forsey; Terry Gabbey (AFA); Luigi
    Galante (Virgil Pomfret
    Agency); Maureen
    Hallahan (B.L. Kearley)
    lettering; Tony Kenyon
    (B.L. Kearley) all cartoons;
    Angus McBride (Linden
    Artists); Nicki Palin.

CONTENTS

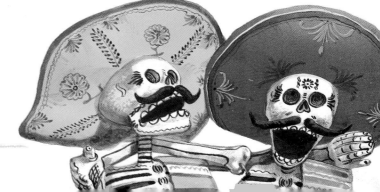

What is a country?

A country is an independent land with its own government. The government runs the country, and makes laws which the people must keep. A country has its own name, and its borders are normally agreed by other countries around the world.

● Each country has its own money, called currency, with its own style of coins and bills. There are rubles in Russia and francs in France.

● All countries have their own stamps, which often carry a picture of the country's ruler. Some stamps show a country's wildlife, or mark an important discovery.

● People wave their national flags at parades, sports events, and celebrations.

CHINA

BRAZIL

SWEDEN

GREECE

GERMANY

ISRAEL

Why do countries fly flags?

Every country has its own flag, which is a sort of national emblem. Each country's flag is different. The design may include colored stripes, star and sun patterns, or religious signs such as crosses or crescents. Flags are flown on special occasions, as a symbol of a country and its people.

● Every country has its own special song called a national anthem. This is sung to show respect for a country and its history.

SUDAN

AUSTRALIA

UNITED KINGDOM

CANADA

TURKEY

ARGENTINA

SOUTH KOREA

JAMAICA

AUSTRIA

Which country has the most people?

Well over a billion people live in China, and about 48,000 new babies are born there every day. You'd think that meant a lot of birthdays, but in China everyone celebrates their birthday at the same time— the Chinese New Year!

● Chinese New Year is celebrated by Chinese people all over the world in late January or early February. There are spectacular street processions.

● In July 1991, both the U.S.A. *and* Canada celebrated their birthdays—over 75,000 people showed up to a huge party, held in the U.S.A.

Which is the biggest country?

Russia is so big it takes eight days to cross it by train! As children set off for school in the capital, Moscow, in the west, others are already going home in the eastern port of Vladivostok.

MOSCOW

VLADIVOSTOK

Where is there land, but no countries?

The vast frozen land around the South Pole is called Antarctica. It is not a country—it has no people, no government, and no flag. Many countries have signed an agreement promising to keep Antarctica as a wilderness for scientists to study.

● Nobody lives in Antarctica except for a few hundred scientists, who go there to study rocks, the weather, and plant and animal life.

How many countries are there?

There are about 190 independent countries in the world, but the number changes from year to year. This is because new countries are sometimes made, or two countries may join together, as East and West Germany did in 1990.

CANADA

UNITED STATES

ATLANTIC OCEAN

MEXICO

PACIFIC OCEAN

CAPE VERDE

ST. CHRISTOPHER & NEVIS

ST. LUCIA

GRENADA

VENEZUELA

GUYANA

SURINAM

COLOMBIA

PERU

BRAZIL

BOLIVIA

PARAGUAY

CHILE

ARGENTINA

URUGUAY

1 Guatemala
2 Belize
3 El Salvador
4 Honduras
5 Nicaragua
6 Costa Rica
7 Panama
8 Cuba
9 Bahamas
10 Jamaica
11 Haiti
12 Dominican Republic
13 Antigua and Barbuda
14 Dominica
15 Barbados
16 St. Vincent and the Grenadines
17 Trinidad and Tobago
18 Ecuador
19 Ireland
20 United Kingdom
21 Belgium
22 Netherlands
23 Luxembourg

24 Switzerland
25 Liechtenstein
26 San Marino
27 Vatican City
28 Italy
29 Monaco
30 Andorra
31 Denmark
32 Estonia
33 Latvia
34 Lithuania
35 Czech Republic
36 Austria
37 Slovakia
38 Hungary
39 Slovenia
40 Croatia
41 Bosnia and Herzogovina
42 Yugoslavia
43 Macedonia
44 Albania
45 Greece
46 Bulgaria
47 Moldova

48 Malta
49 Cyprus
50 Lebanon
51 Israel
52 Jordan
53 Armenia
54 Azerbaijan
55 Kuwait
56 Bahrain
57 Qatar
58 United Arab Emirates

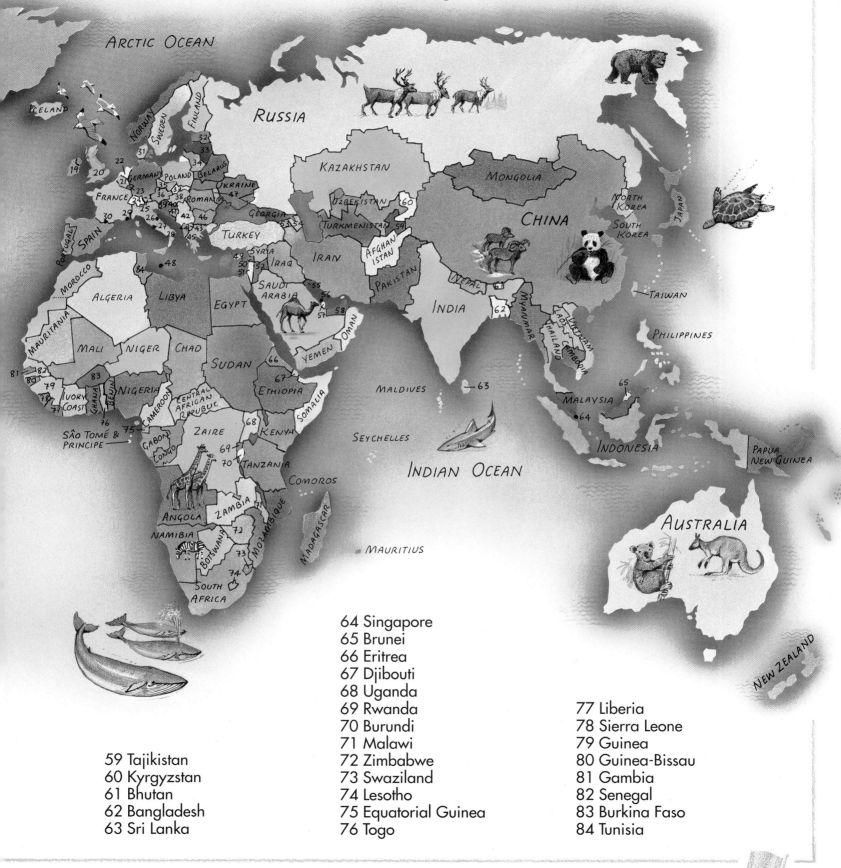

● Some small Pacific island countries are not shown on this map: Fiji, Kiribati, Marshall Islands, Federated States of Micronesia, Nauru, Palau, Tonga, Tuvalu, and Western Samoa.

ARCTIC OCEAN

ICELAND

NORWAY
SWEDEN
FINLAND

RUSSIA

19
20
22
31
32
33
34

GERMANY
POLAND
BELARUS
UKRAINE

FRANCE
21
23
35
37
36
38
24
25
89
40
41
42
46
47
30
29
26
27
28
43
44
45

PORTUGAL
SPAIN

GEORGIA

KAZAKHSTAN

MONGOLIA

CHINA

NORTH KOREA
SOUTH KOREA

JAPAN

TAIWAN

PHILIPPINES

TURKEY

UZBEKISTAN
60
TURKMENISTAN
59
53
54

IRAN
AFGHANISTAN

MOROCCO

ALGERIA
LIBYA
EGYPT
84
48

SYRIA
49
50
52
51
IRAQ

55
56
57
58

SAUDI ARABIA
PAKISTAN

NEPAL
61

INDIA

62

MYANMAR

LAOS
THAILAND
VIETNAM
CAMBODIA

MAURITANIA
MALI
NIGER
CHAD
SUDAN
66
67
ETHIOPIA

YEMEN
OMAN

MALDIVES
63

MALAYSIA
65
64

81
82
80
79
83
78
IVORY COAST
77
76
GHANA
BENIN
NIGERIA
CAMEROON
CENTRAL AFRICAN REPUBLIC
68
KENYA
SOMALIA

SEYCHELLES

INDONESIA

PAPUA NEW GUINEA

SÃO TOMÉ & PRINCIPE
75
GABON
CONGO
ZAIRE
69
70
TANZANIA

COMOROS

INDIAN OCEAN

ANGOLA
ZAMBIA
71
MADAGASCAR

MAURITIUS

AUSTRALIA

NAMIBIA
BOTSWANA
72
73
MOZAMBIQUE
74

SOUTH AFRICA

NEW ZEALAND

64 Singapore
65 Brunei
66 Eritrea
67 Djibouti
68 Uganda
69 Rwanda
70 Burundi
71 Malawi
72 Zimbabwe
73 Swaziland
74 Lesotho
75 Equatorial Guinea
76 Togo

59 Tajikistan
60 Kyrgyzstan
61 Bhutan
62 Bangladesh
63 Sri Lanka

77 Liberia
78 Sierra Leone
79 Guinea
80 Guinea-Bissau
81 Gambia
82 Senegal
83 Burkina Faso
84 Tunisia

Which city is above the clouds?

The city of Lhasa is in Tibet, a part of China. It is built near the edge of the Himalayas, the world's highest mountains. Lhasa is so high that it's often covered by clouds, which blanket the city in a thick wet mist!

● Some people call Tibet the Roof of the World, because it so high up in the mountains.

Why do Venetians walk on water?

The Italian city of Venice is built on dozens of tiny islands in a sheltered lagoon near the sea. In between the islands are canals, which form the main "streets" of the city. To get from one part of Venice to another, you don't take a bus or a train —you catch a motorboat or a gondola.

● You have to climb 1,000 steps to reach the Potala Palace, which towers above the streets of Lhasa. It's very grand —even its roofs are made of gold!

● A country's capital city is where the government works. Washington, D.C. is the capital of the U.S.A. The president lives there, in the White House.

Which is the world's biggest city?

Over 21 million people live in Mexico's capital. Mexico City is already home to more people than the whole of Australia, and it's growing fast!

Who writes with a paintbrush?

In China and Japan handwriting can be an art. Instead of writing with a pen, people sometimes paint words slowly and beautifully with a brush and ink. Artists often frame their written work, and hang it on the wall just like a picture.

● About 50,000 different symbols may be used to write Chinese. Luckily, schoolchildren only have to learn about 5,000 of them.

● The art of beautiful handwriting is called calligraphy. Japanese children learn calligraphy at school.

Who reads back-to-front?

To read a book in Arabic or Hebrew, you have to work from right to left. So if this book were in Arabic, the first page would be where the index is now.

Which country speaks over 800 languages?

Papua New Guinea is a land of many languages. Most of the people live in small villages, deep in the rain forest or high up in the misty mountains. Some are so cut off from each other that their languages are quite different.

● In many areas of Papua New Guinea, people can only talk to each other through a translator.

Jambo! — Swahili
Namaste! — Hindi
¡Hola! — Spanish
Czesc! — Polish
Dag! — Dutch

● Around 5,000 languages are spoken throughout the world. Here are just a few ways to say "hello."

● There's a place in New Zealand with 85 letters in its name. And there's another in France with just one!

Taumatawhakatangihangakoauauotamateaturipukakapikimaungahoronukupokaiwhenuakitanatahu

Who lives in a longhouse?

On the tropical island of Borneo, some people live in long, airy buildings that are made of wood and bamboo, and are raised on stilts. These longhouses are home to dozens of different families, each with their own room.

● As many as 100 families may share the same longhouse.

● High-rise apartment buildings are another way of squeezing a lot of homes into a small space. You find them in big towns and cities.

Where do gardens grow on rivers?

In the Netherlands, many people live on barges moored on the country's canals. Boat-owners don't have backyards, of course, but some of them grow flowers on the roof!

How do you stay cozy in the Gobi?

The Gobi Desert is in Mongolia in northern Asia and its winters are icy cold. Some shepherds and their families travel around the desert, living in thick, felt tents called yurts, which keep out the hot sun or the freezing cold.

Which is the oldest dish on the menu?

● All over the world, people pound grains such as corn to make flour for their pancakes.

Pancakes may be the oldest dish of all. Even Stone Age people baked them! The basic recipe—milk, eggs, and flour—is the same the world over, but the kind of flour changes from place to place. Pancakes can be made using flour from potatoes, corn, wheat, or oats.

● In different parts of the world you might find almost anything on your plate—from crunchy insects or chewy snails to snakes, guinea pigs, or even sheep's eyes!

Who eats shells, butterflies, and little worms?

• Table manners vary from place to place. We think it is impolite to put your elbows on the table at dinner, while the French think it's perfectly all right!

We do! These are all types of pasta—their Italian names are *conchiglie* (kon-**chil**-ee—shells), *farfalle* (far-**fal**-ay—butterflies), and *vermicelli* (vur-me-**chel**-ee—little worms). Pasta is a dough made from flour and water, which is cut into shapes and then boiled.

Vermicelli

Farfalle

Conchiglie

• Pasta dough comes in more than 100 shapes and sizes including stars, snail shapes, and all the letters of the alphabet.

Where does it take all afternoon to have a cup of tea?

In Japan there's a special ancient tea ceremony called *chanoyu* (cha-**noy**-yu). The tea is made so slowly, and sipped so carefully, that it really does take hours. It's not a good idea to show up feeling thirsty!

Where do women wear bowler hats?

● Lake Titicaca, in the Andes Mountains is the highest lake in the world. The people there use reed boats to travel between islands.

In the Andes Mountains of South America, many women wear bowler hats. The hat is now a part of their traditional dress, along with full skirts, brightly-colored llama (**la**-ma)-wool shawls, and ponchos.

● Bowler hats were first made for men, not women! British businessmen began wearing them to work over 100 years ago.

Where do men wear skirts?

On special occasions in the Highlands of Scotland, it's traditional for men to wear kilts. These pleated skirts are made of a woolen, plaid cloth called tartan. Kilts are warm, but they only come down to the knee, so they are worn with a pair of long, woolen socks.

Which dress has no stitches?

The Indian sari is a simple length of cloth, that wraps neatly around a woman's body. It has no stitching, buttons, or zippers and its design hasn't really changed for hundreds of years. Saris are made of bright cottons or shimmering silks, and on a hot day they are very cool and comfortable to wear.

● People who live in desert countries traditionally wear long robes and head cloths to protect them from the heat and dust. In Arctic countries people wrap up warmly in fur-lined parkas.

● In Scotland, each family group has its own tartan, with a particular pattern and color.

Who wears money at a wedding?

At a Greek or Turkish wedding, the guests don't take the bride and groom gifts —they take money instead. At the wedding party, this is pinned all over the couple's clothes. Often there is so much money that they are both completely covered.

● On the island of Madagascar, a man makes a speech to his bride-to-be before she'll marry him. If the speech is no good, he pays a fine and starts again!

● Hindu brides decorate their skin with beautiful, lacy patterns for their wedding day. They use a reddish-brown dye called henna.

Where are children made kings and queens?

On January 6, French families enjoy a special dinner together.
   At the end of the meal, the children eat slices of a flat almond pie called a *galette* (ga-**let**). In one slice a charm is hidden. Whoever finds it is crowned king or queen for the night.

● Three kings from the East are said to have visited the two-week-old infant Jesus on January 6.

Who sticks out their tongue to say "hello"?

One of the customs of the Maori people of New Zealand is to welcome important guests by staring at them fiercely, and sticking out their tongues— not something you should try unless you're a Maori!

Where do children watch shadows?

Shadow puppet shows are enjoyed by people all over the world. On the Indonesian island of Java, the audience sits on both sides of a cloth screen. One side watches the puppets, the other sees the shadows dance, as if by magic!

● Javanese puppets are made of painted leather. The puppeteer moves them with wires or rods.

● In a Vietnamese water puppet show, the story is acted out on the surface of a lake. It can't be much fun for the puppeteers— they have to stand in the water.

Who makes pictures from sand?

The Navajo people of the southwestern United States create beautiful pictures with grains of colored sand. The pictures are made on the ground for special ceremonies. But these works of art don't last long— they are destroyed afterward!

● Some sand pictures are said to have healing powers and are big enough to allow the sick person to sit in the middle of them.

● In Switzerland, cow herders used to play alpenhorns— long wooden horns that echoed from one mountain to another.

Which dancers snap their fingers?

Flamenco dancing comes from southern Spain. Proud-looking dancers toss their heads and snap their fingers, as they stamp and whirl to the music of a Spanish guitar.

Where are wheat fields bigger than countries?

The rolling grasslands of Canada and the United States are planted with wheat as far as the eye can see. One Canadian wheat field was so big, it was double the size of the European country San Marino!

● Huge combine harvesters have to work in teams to harvest the gigantic wheat fields.

● More people eat rice than wheat. Rice plants need to stand in water, and are grown on flooded land called paddies.

Where does chocolate grow on trees?

Chocolate is made from the seeds of the cacao (ka-**cow**) tree. These trees don't grow every-where—just in the hot, wet parts of South America, Southeast Asia, and West Africa.

Which country has more sheep than people?

● In Thailand, coconut farmers train monkeys to harvest their crop. The monkeys scamper up the trunks of the palm trees and throw down the fruits.

Although there are more than 17 million people in Australia, most live around the coast. In the center people run enormous sheep farms. At the last count, there were 147 million sheep— nearly nine times the number of people!

Who rides on a snowmobile?

Many of the people who live in icy parts of North America travel across the frozen snow on powerful sleds called snowmobiles. Not long ago, sleds were pulled by husky dogs, but now these are only raced for fun.

- A dog team can pull a sled about 50 miles in a day. A snowmobile covers that distance in an hour.

- Trains in Tokyo, Japan, are so crowded that railroad staff called crushers have to push in the passengers while the doors close.

- Fishermen in Portugal paint "magic" eyes on their boats to watch over them at sea and bring them safely to harbor.

Where do you park your bike in China?

There are millions and millions of people in China, and many millions of bikes! All Chinese cities have huge parking lots for bikes. An attendant gives your bike a number, and helps you to find it again later.

Who paints pictures on trucks?

The truck drivers of Afghanistan are very proud of their trucks. They paint pictures all over them, covering every last inch with bright, colorful patterns. Even the wheel nuts are painted different colors.

● The Afghans may drape their trucks with silver chains and even stick on ring-pulls from soda cans as decorations.

27

Why do people race camels?

One-humped camels are so sturdy and fast that in hot desert areas they are ridden like racehorses. The races are very popular in Saudi Arabia, and large crowds cheer the camels as they speed across desert racetracks.

● Dromedaries can race at over 12 miles an hour—faster than two-humped camels.

● People have been known to race all sorts and sizes of animal—from ostriches to snails!

● The world's fastest ball game is called pelota. The ball is hurled from a wicker scoop at the speed of an express train.

Which is the world's most popular sport?

Soccer balls are kicked around in more than 160 countries around the world. The game is played in playgrounds, parks, streets and, of course, soccer fields.

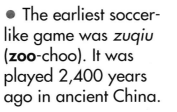

● The earliest soccer-like game was *zuqiu* (**zoo**-choo). It was played 2,400 years ago in ancient China.

Where do elephants glow in the dark?

For the Sri Lankan festival of the Esala Perahera, elephants are decorated with beautiful hangings and strings of electric lights. More than 50 elephants take part in a nighttime procession, along with thousands of drummers and dancers, who crack whips and wave colorful banners.

● The leprechaun (**lep-re-kon**) of Irish folktales is a little green man. The green shamrock is Ireland's national flower.

When do people eat green food?

Saint Patrick is the patron saint of Ireland, and green is the country's national color. Saint Patrick's Day falls on March 17, and for Irish people everywhere it's a time of wild celebration. Some people even dye party food green!

When is the Day of the Dead?

The Day of the Dead is a Mexican holiday which takes place every year on November 2, All Souls' Day. People remember dead friends and relatives by taking flowers and candles to their graves, and having picnics there.

● Brightly painted fake skeletons are made for the Day of the Dead celebrations.

● February is carnival time in many countries, with glittering parades and music.

● The Esala Perahera procession takes place in Kandy, Sri Lanka, at the time of the July full moon.

Index

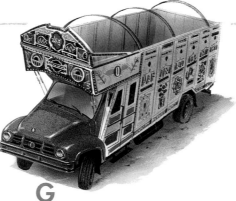

32